First hundred words in French

colouring book

At the bottom of each page are little pictures of objects, with the French word for them written underneath. Look for the objects in the big pictures and colour them in. There is a little yellow duck to find in every picture, too. When you have found it, colour it in, then finish colouring the picture.

Le salon
The living room

Papa
Daddy

Maman
Mummy

le garçon
boy

la fille

girl

le bébé

baby

le chien

dog

le chat

cat

3

Les vêtements
Clothes

les chaussures

shoes

la culotte

pants

le tee-shirt

t-shirt

4

le maillot de corps
vest

le pantalon
trousers

le pull
jumper

les chaussettes
socks

5

Le petit déjeuner

Breakfast

le pain

bread

le lait

milk

les oeufs

eggs

la pomme
apple

l'orange
orange

la banane
banana

Les jouets
Toys

le cheval
horse

le mouton
sheep

la vache
cow

8

la poule
hen

le cochon
pig

le train
train

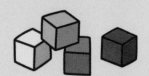
les cubes
bricks

9

Dans la cuisine

In the kitchen

la table
table

la chaise
chair

l'assiette
plate

10

le couteau
knife

la fourchette
fork

la cuillère
spoon

la tasse
cup

11

Chez Grand-mère et Grand-père

At Granny and Grandpa's house

Grand-mère
Granny

Grand-père
Grandpa

les pantoufles
slippers

le manteau
coat

la robe
dress

le chapeau
hat

13

Au jardin public

In the park

14

l'arbre
tree

la fleur
flower

les balançoires
swings

la balle
ball

le toboggan
slide

les bottes
boots

l'oiseau
bird

le bateau
boat

Dans la rue

In the street

la voiture
car

le vélo
bicycle

l'avion
plane

le camion
truck

l'autobus
bus

la maison
house

17

La fête

The party

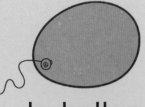

le ballon

balloon

le gâteau

cake

la pendule

clock

18

la glace
ice cream

le poisson
fish

les biscuits
biscuits

les bonbons
sweets

19

A la piscine

At the swimming pool

le bras

arm

la main

hand

les orteils

toes

les pieds
feet

la jambe
leg

la tête
head

le derrière
bottom

21

Au vestiaire
In the changing room

la bouche
mouth

les yeux
eyes

les oreilles
ears

le nez
nose

les cheveux
hair

le peigne
comb

la brosse
brush

Dans le magasin

In the shop

rouge
red

bleu
blue

vert
green

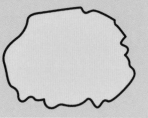
jaune
yellow

rose
pink

blanc
white

noir
black

25

Dans la salle de bains

In the bathroom

le savon
soap

la serviette
towel

les toilettes
toilet

le bain
bath

le ventre
tummy

le canard
duck

27

Dans la chambre

In the bedroom

le lit
bed

la lampe
lamp

la fenêtre
window

 **la porte**
door

 **le livre**
book

 **la poupée**
doll

 **l'ours**
teddy

29

Les nombres

Numbers

1 un / une
one

2 deux
two

3 trois
three

4 quatre
four

5 cinq
five

| **1 un / une** | **2 deux** | **3 trois** | **4 quatre** | **5 cinq** |
| one | two | three | four | five |

30

Word list

In this alphabetical list of all the words in the pictures, the French word comes first, next is the guide to saying the word, and then there is the English translation. The guide may look strange or funny, but just try to read the words as if they were English. It will help you to say the words in French correctly, if you remember these rules:

g is said like **g** in **g**ame

j is said like **s** in trea**s**ure

r is made by growling a little at the back of your throat

n at the end of a word is said at the back of your nose.
There is no sound like it in English

a sounds halfway between the **a** in c**a**t and the **a** in c**a**r

ay is like the **ay** in d**ay**

l'arbre (m)	*lar-br*	tree
l'assiette (f)	*lass-ee-et*	plate
l'autobus (m)	*lo-toe-bews*	bus
l'avion (m)	*lav-yon*	plane
le bain	*le ban*	bath
les balançoires (f)	*lay bal-on-swar*	swings
la balle	*la bal*	ball
le ballon	*le ba-lon*	balloon
la banane	*la ba-nan*	banana
le bateau	*le ba-toe*	boat
le bébé	*le bay-bay*	baby
les biscuits (m)	*lay beess-kwee*	biscuits
blanc	*blon*	white
bleu	*bler*	blue
les bonbons (m)	*lay bon-bon*	sweets
les bottes (f)	*lay bot*	boots
la bouche	*la boosh*	mouth
le bras	*le bra*	arm
la brosse	*la bross*	brush
le camion	*le ka-mee-on*	truck
le canard	*le ka-nar*	duck
la chaise	*la shayz*	chair
la chambre	*la shom-br*	bedroom
le chapeau	*le sha-poe*	hat
le chat	*le sha*	cat
les chaussettes (f)	*lay show-set*	socks
les chaussures (f)	*lay show-sewr*	shoes
le cheval	*le sher-val*	horse
les cheveux (m)	*lay sher-ver*	hair
le chien	*le shee-an*	dog
cinq	*sank*	five
le cochon	*le cosh-on*	pig
le couteau	*le coo-toe*	knife
les cubes (m)	*lay kewb*	bricks
la cuillère	*la kwee-yair*	spoon
la cuisine	*la kwee-zeen*	kitchen
la culotte	*la kew-lot*	pants
le derrière	*le dare-ee-air*	bottom
deux	*der*	two
la fenêtre	*la fe-netr*	window
la fête	*la fet*	party
la fille	*la fee-ye*	girl
la fleur	*la fler*	flower
la fourchette	*la foor-shet*	fork
le garçon	*le gar-sonn*	boy
le gâteau	*le ga-toe*	cake
la glace	*la glass*	ice cream
Grand-mère	*gron-mair*	Granny
Grand-père	*gron-pair*	Grandpa
la jambe	*la jomb*	leg
le jardin public	*le jar-dan poo-bleek*	park
jaune	*jone*	yellow
les jouets (m)	*lay joo-ay*	toys
le lait	*le lay*	milk
la lampe	*la lomp*	lamp

le lit	*le lee*	bed	la porte	*la por-t*	door
le livre	*le lee-vr*	book	la poule	*la pool*	hen
			la poupée	*la poo-pay*	doll
le magasin	*le ma-ga-zan*	shop	le pull	*le pewl*	jumper
le maillot	*le my-o*	vest			
de corps	*de cor*		quatre	*ka-tr*	four
la main	*la man*	hand			
la maison	*la may-zon*	house	la robe	*la rob*	dress
Maman	*ma-mon*	Mummy	rose	*rose*	pink
le manteau	*le mon-toe*	coat	rouge	*rooj*	red
le mouton	*le moo-ton*	sheep	la rue	*la roo*	street
le nez	*le nay*	nose	la salle de bains	*la sal de ban*	bathroom
noir	*nwar*	black	le salon	*le salon*	living
les nombres	*lay nom-br*	numbers			room
(m)			le savon	*le sa-von*	soap
			la serviette	*la sair-vee-et*	towel
l'oeuf (m)	*lerf*	egg			
les oeufs (m)	*lay zer*	eggs	la table	*la ta-bl*	table
l'oiseau (m)	*lwa-zoe*	bird	la tasse	*la tass*	cup
l'orange (f)	*lor-onj*	orange	le tee-shirt	*le tee-shirt*	t-shirt
les oreilles (f)	*lay zor-ay*	ears	la tête	*la tet*	head
les orteils (m)	*lay zor-tay*	toes	le toboggan	*le tob-og-on*	slide
l'ours (m)	*loorce*	teddy	les toilettes (f)	*lay twal-et*	toilet
			le train	*le tran*	train
le pain	*le pan*	bread	trois	*trwa*	three
le pantalon	*le pon-ta-lon*	trousers			
les pantoufles	*lay pon-too-fl*	slippers	un (m) / une (f)	*an / oon*	one
(f)			la vache	*la vash*	cow
Papa	*pa-pa*	Daddy	le vélo	*le vay-lo*	bicycle
le peigne	*le payn-ye*	comb	le ventre	*le von-tr*	tummy
la pendule	*la pon-dewl*	clock	vert	*vair*	green
le petit	*le pe-tee*		le vestiaire	*le*	changing
déjeuner	*day-je-nay*	breakfast		*vays-tee-air*	room
les pieds (m)	*lay pee-ay*	feet	les vêtements	*lay vet-mon*	clothes
la piscine	*la pee-seen*	swimming	(m)		
		pool	la voiture	*la vwa-tewr*	car
le poisson	*le pwa-sonn*	fish			
la pomme	*la pomm*	apple	les yeux (m)	*layz-yer*	eyes

Written by Heather Amery
Translated by Nicole Irving
Based on illustrations by Stephen Cartwright
Designed by Mike Olley and Jan McCafferty
Digital manipulation by Lizzie Barber

First published in 2009 by Usborne Publishing Ltd, Usborne House, 83-85 Saffron Hill, London EC1N 8RT, England. www.usborne.com